HANUKKAH:
EIGHT LIGHTS AROUND THE WORLD

Susan Sussman
Illustrations by Judith Friedman

Albert Whitman & Company, Niles, Illinois

I would love to have traveled around the world to research
this book. In a way I have, through the knowledge, experiences,
and memories of: Rabbi Michael Azose; Rita Brezka; Caroline
Goldenstein; Yael and Avi Hanani; David Harris, American Jewish
Committee; Rabbi Ezekiel Musleah; Rabbi Arnold Rachlis; Shelly
Waitsman Riskin; Jacques Sapriel; Professor Norman A. Stillman;
Marilyn Tallman, Chicago Action for Soviet Jewry; Rabbi Henry
Toledano; Flora Yavelberg; and Richard Zelin, Chicago Conference
on Soviet Jewry. Thank you all for your generosity of time and spirit.

I am grateful to Kathleen Tucker at Albert Whitman for urging me
to think, once again, about Hanukkah, and to my editor, Abby
Levine, whose care and concern enrich each page of this book.

Library of Congress Cataloging-in-Publication Data

Sussman, Susan.
   Hanukkah: eight lights around the world.

   *Summary: Eight short stories depict eight
contemporary Jewish families in different countries
celebrating the holiday.*
   *1. Hanukkah—Juvenile fiction. 2. Children's
stories, American. [1. Hanukkah—Fiction. 2. Short
stories] I. Friedman, Judith, 1945—   ill.*
II. Title
PZ7.S9657Han 1988   [Fic]   87-25346
ISBN 0-8075-3145-6 (lib. bdg.)

The Story of Hanukkah

Two thousand years ago, Israel fell under the rule of King Antiochus of Syria. He decreed that everyone in the land must worship Greek gods and idols. The Jews refused, saying they worshipped but one God. This angered the king. He would force the Jews to obey!

Antiochus outlawed Jewish ceremonies and rituals. Parents who had their sons circumcised were killed. People refusing to eat foods forbidden by Jewish law were executed. The king rededicated the Temple in Jerusalem to the Greek god Zeus. Sacred bowls, vessels, and oil were used in ceremonies where swine and other animals were sacrificed on the altar. The Temple was defiled.

Outside Jerusalem, in a town called Modin, lived a religious leader named Mattathias. He and his five sons continued to practice Judaism. The king sent soldiers to Modin. Jews were told to make sacrifices to Zeus. When one man stepped forward to do this, Mattathias became so enraged that he killed both the offender and the king's commissioner. Mattathias and his sons then fled into the hills of Modin, where they continued to practice their religion. Many Jews heard about Mattathias and joined his family.

Antiochus ordered his soldiers to kill the Jews of Modin. A long and difficult struggle began. Mattathias died during these years, and his son, the great warrior Judah Maccabee, became leader. Judah taught his followers—people who had been farmers, merchants, laborers—

to become warriors. Jews continued to come from all over the land, and Judah shaped them into an army. For three years they fought skirmishes with the king's soldiers. Finally, Judah felt his people were ready to come down from the hills and fight for their Temple.

The Jews were greatly outnumbered by their enemy, but they fought fiercely. The Syrians fled, and the Jews reclaimed the Temple in Jerusalem. They cleaned out the filth, restoring the Temple to its former beauty. A new altar was built. The Jews said prayers and performed rituals that rededicated the Temple to God. Judah declared the rejoicing should last eight days, beginning the twenty-fifth day of the month of Kislev, the third anniversary of Antiochus's decree. The holiday was named Hanukkah, which means "dedication."

This account of Hanukkah was written by a Maccabee soon after the events took place. But the story we know best, the one about the miracle of the oil, did not appear until several centuries later, in writings called the Gemara. Here, rabbis tell how the Maccabees prepared to celebrate the dedication of the Temple by lighting the menorah. Only one small jar of sacred oil could be found, barely enough to last a single day. The light would die out before more oil could be purified. Then a great miracle happened. Instead of burning one day, the oil burned for eight!

Today, Jews all over the world kindle the Hanukkah lights. In every culture, families gather to recount the courage of the Maccabees and the miracle of the oil. Each year, Hanukkah serves as a reminder that the freedom to worship as we choose is a precious right, a right all the people of this world must keep alive. Forever.

The First Night: Israel

Shlomo grips his father's hand and waits. In the hills far above, a huge bonfire blazes red against the morning sky. Runners touch torches to the flames and lift them high. One by one, they start their run down the hills of Modin. The Freedom Torch Relay begins.

"Look," says Father as a runner comes toward them. "Can this be the great warrior Judah Maccabee?"

Shlomo looks, then laughs. "That's Avi, the butcher's son."

"Perhaps you're right," says Father. "But long ago, this very place was the home of the Maccabees. Those brave warriors stood on these hills, lived in these caves, while they fought for the freedom to worship as they pleased. In fact, I think the mighty Judah once stood exactly where you stand now."

Shlomo looks down. Is that the print of an ancient sandal under his foot?

"Ready?" asks Father. Shlomo does not feel ready. What if he cannot keep up? What if he falls? His heart pounds as Avi comes to them and lights Father's torch with his. "Ready?" Father asks again.

"Yes," says Shlomo, his voice a whisper.

They begin running. Shlomo has practiced many weeks for this. Each day before dinner, he and Father ran near their home in Jerusalem. Each day Shlomo was able to go a little farther than the time before. Now he keeps pace down the road that winds through the hills of Modin. Running downhill is not so hard. Still, Shlomo is glad he does not have to run the whole seventeen miles to Jerusalem.

A young soldier waits at the next station. She smiles as Shlomo helps Father pass the torch's flame. Before this day ends, torches lit in Modin will be carried throughout Israel so people everywhere can see the flame of freedom.

Shlomo and his father return to Jerusalem. At sundown, their family joins the excited crowd around a giant hanukkiyah. Everyone cheers as the light of the first Freedom Relay torch appears in the distance. One by one, runners arrive and throw their torches into a pile to make a great fire. The last torch is used to light the shammash, the helper candle, which then lights the first light of Hanukkah. It is the twenty-fifth of the month of Kislev. Hanukkah has begun.

At home, Shlomo and his family sing the blessings as his mother lights the first Hanukkah candle. Shlomo and his sister, Tamar, take turns telling the Hanukkah story.

"The ancient Temple was taken from the Jews," says Tamar. "Our enemies brought pigs and idols into the Temple. There were many enemies, and we had few warriors. But Judah and the Maccabees were brave. They came down from Modin and drove our enemies out of the Temple."

Now it is Shlomo's turn. "The Maccabees cleaned the Temple," he says. "Then they needed sacred oil to make the Temple holy again. A small jar of the oil was found hidden. It was only enough to burn for one day, but it burned for eight."

"Well done! Well done!" Mother and Father clap their hands. Shlomo and Tamar bow. Mother sets an old record of holiday music on the turntable and plays the Hanukkah songs. Tamar dances a folk dance she learned in school, then has everyone try it. The steps are easy, and Shlomo learns quickly.

It has been a long day. Shlomo's legs are weary as he climbs into bed. From his window he sees Hanukkah lights flicker in the windows of other homes. As he sleeps, he dreams of the time he will be strong enough to run with the torch. One day he will carry the flame with his children, and with his children's children. With their help, he will keep Judah Maccabee's two-thousand-year-old light of freedom burning. Forever.

The Second Night: Mexico

Mahalel turns left instead of right on his way to school. These eight days, he leaves his house early to make a special stop. Ducking down a narrow street, he zippers his thin jacket against the December chill. Was his home in Syria ever this cold? Was his home in Syria—? Mahalel stops himself. His mother says Mexico City is their home now. He must get used to it.

The small synagogue waits at the end of the street. Mahalel pushes against the heavy wood door and steps inside. It takes a moment for his eyes to adjust from the bright sun to the soft light of the room. He smells the burning wicks before he sees their glow. Mahalel walks down the aisle to the bimah. Twelve oil lamps flicker on the tiny stage to honor the twelve tribes of Israel. An old rabbi looks up from his prayerbook and smiles. Like Mahalel, the rabbi has fled to Mexico from Syria.

An ancient hanukkiyah stands ready on the bimah. Hanukkah has special meaning for Mahalel. What could be more important than a holiday celebrating freedom of religion? He doesn't expect his new friends to understand. They say Hanukkah is not nearly as much fun as Purim, when they get to wear costumes and put on plays. But they've lived in Mexico all their lives. They never had to flee their homes and move to an unfamiliar land just because they were Jewish.

A few men come into the synagogue. Mahalel likes the hum of their voices as they pray. He wants to stay longer, but school will begin soon. It is hard for him to leave the synagogue. The oil lamps and the old rabbi fill him with memories of the home he left behind.

The day goes well. Mahalel has a funny part in the class play and makes everyone laugh. Mexico doesn't seem quite so strange now that he is able to speak and understand Spanish a little better. Friends invite him to join their soccer game after school. He plays late into the afternoon until it is time to go home.

This night it is Mahalel's turn to pour oil into the hanukkiyah. There are places for eight lights on the bottom row and two lights on the top. Mahalel pours oil into two bottom holders for the second night of Hanukkah. Then he fills the two top holders, the shammashim. His father lights the oil wicks.

"Most Jews," says his father, "have but one shammash light. But Jews from our part of Syria light two. This second light helps us to remember our ancestors, who were forced from Spain in 1492 because they were Jews. Country after country turned them away. When at last Syria took them in, they vowed to light a second shammash to give thanks to the Almighty for their new home."

Mahalel frowns. "But now the Syrians don't want us," he says. "Why do we still light two shammashim?"

"Tradition," says Father. "Besides, now that we're safe in this country, we can let the second shammash stand for Mexico. It can be our way of giving thanks to the Almighty for this fine new home."

Mahalel's gift this Hanukkah is a beautiful candle shaped like a hand. His grandmother says the hand will protect him from the "evil eye," those bad thoughts or feelings people might have against him. Mahalel doesn't exactly believe in this old superstition. But it can't hurt to hang the candle on the wall over his bed. Perhaps the hand will keep his new home safe from the "evil eye" that drove him from Syria. Perhaps he and his family will be able to stay in Mexico. Forever.

The Third Night: Argentina

"Ouch!" Carola scrapes her knuckles against the grater, again. "I'm grating more finger than potato!"

"Don't try to use up every little bit," says her mother. "I have plenty of potatoes, but you have only ten fingers!"

Carola breaks an egg into the bowl and picks out a little piece of shell. Her mother adds onion, flour, and salt. While Carola mixes everything together, her mother sets two large frying pans on the stove. Carola pours a little oil into each pan. The oil reminds her of the miracle of the Hanukkah oil that burned for eight days.

When the oil is hot, Mother spoons circles of batter into the pans. The oil bubbles and sizzles, spattering into the air. Carola wants to cook, but the oil pricks her arms like hot needles. She helps by spreading paper towels on top of newspapers. As soon as the potato batter cooks into crisp brown pancakes, Mother lifts the latkes onto the toweling to drain.

Father comes home from his office. His shirt, so clean and neat this morning, is wet and wrinkled from the hot drive home. He gives a big kiss to Mother and a little kiss to Carola, then goes into the other room to rest.

Sundown is not until nine o'clock tonight. There is plenty of time to set a proper Sabbath table. Carola spreads out her favorite white cloth and carefully folds the matching napkins into triangles. Next come the dishes, glasses, silver, and two candlesticks.

Now for the job that's most fun of all. Carola takes the straw basket and pruning shears out to the yard. The summer garden this December is a great clash of colors: reds and oranges, purples and pinks. Surely it is the brightest garden in all Buenos Aires! Carola snips the flowers, picking off ants and shooing away bees until her basket is full. Back in the house, she fills two vases with bouquets and sets them on the table.

This year, the third night of Hanukkah falls on Friday, the beginning of the Sabbath. Once the Sabbath candles are burning, no other candles may be lit, so Carola and her family light the Hanukkah candles first. On this Sabbath night only, Hanukkah gifts are given before sundown.

Father holds two fists out over the table. "Choose one," he says. Carola touches his left hand. Slowly, so slowly, he unfolds his fingers. Nothing. Quickly, she touches his right hand. This time, three australs drop out.

"Thank you," she says, hugging her father. She puts the

Hanukkah money in her little bank. Then, as they do every Friday night, Carola and her family light the candles and say the prayers welcoming the Sabbath.

Mother places a crisp roast duck on the table, and Carola proudly carries in the plate of potato pancakes. Her father sprinkles salt on his latkes, but Carola and her mother like to eat theirs with sugar.

As she eats, Carola tells what she will do with the Hanukkah gelt in her bank. Some she will save. Some she will use to buy a pen that writes in four different colors. And some she will add to the pushke, the charity box kept on the kitchen counter. For Carola knows it is both her duty and her blessing to share with those less fortunate. Forever.

The Fourth Night: The United States

Sy and Aaron stick Hanukkah candles into the holders they made at Sunday school. Aaron's class shaped hanukkiyot out of clay. At first Aaron made all nine candle holders the same size. He forgot the shammash had to be taller. The rabbi helped him fix it. Sy glued eight large metal nuts to a strong piece of wood. To make the shammash taller, he glued three nuts together.

Last month, the boys' hanukkiyot were on display at the Spertus Museum in Chicago. Their teachers took them to see the glass cases filled with hanukkiyot from all over the world: gold and silver, bronze and brass, big and small, fancy and plain. Some were many centuries old, and some were new. And in a special section, set out for everyone to see, were the hanukkiyot from Sy and Aaron's school. Aaron was afraid he wouldn't get his back in time for Hanukkah. But he did.

The boys put the hanukkiyot on the table in front of the window. Mother lights the shammash candles and hands them to Sy and Aaron. "Ba-rukh a-tah A-do-nai," they sing as they carefully light the other candles. Mother and Father's strong voices join in the blessing. No one notices when the boys forget a word here and there. Father opens the curtains to let the dancing lights shine out onto the street.

After dinner, Sy and Aaron help clear the table. The family will wash the dishes later. First, there are important matters to be taken care of. They go to the living room in time to see the last flickering of the candles.

Father sits at the piano. Mother sets her guitar on her lap. The boys beat wooden spoons in time to the music. "Hanuk-kah, O Hanukkah, Come Light the Menorah," they sing. Then, "I Had a Little Dreidel" and "Rock of Ages."

Finally, it is time for the Hanukkah presents. Aaron gives everyone a clay dreidel. He has painted each toy top blue and white, the colors of Israel. Sy passes out bookmarks shaped like Hanukkah candles. Each candle is made of cardboard wrapped in gold foil. He has glued red glitter on top for the flames. Father brings out a box of sufganiyot, delicious jelly doughnuts that are fried in oil, then coated with powdered sugar. They all sit on the floor, eating the doughnuts and spinning the dreidels. When everyone has finished eating, Mother licks the sugar from her fingers and places her hands over her eyes.

"I am thinking of a place," she says mysteriously, "a dark, dark place, where boots and coats live—"

"The closet!" shout the boys, jumping up, running to look. They find presents hidden deep in the pockets of Father's coat. Inside the wrappings are bright-colored markers and small pads of paper. The boys draw until bedtime, making Hanukkah pictures to send to Bubbe and Zayde who live far, far away. Pictures their grandparents will keep. Forever.

The Fifth Night: France

Jacques and his friends run through the quiet Sunday streets of Strasbourg, bravely slashing enemies with swords. They are mighty Maccabees on the way to reclaim their Temple. Jacques leads the race across the large square to the Rue de la Paix, the Street of Peace, where the white marble synagogue stands waiting. As always, its two enormous bronze doors are closed. None of the children has ever seen them open.

"My father says this temple is so strong," says Suzanne, who thinks she knows everything, "that even Judah and the Maccabees couldn't have recaptured it."

"If this was Judah's Temple," says Jacques, "it couldn't have been taken in the first place."

The children enter the synagogue through a smaller door. Above them, bronze letters in the white marble say:

STRONGER THAN THE SWORD IS MY SPIRIT.

Jacques's teacher sits with the children in a circle on the floor. "Long ago," she says, spinning a small dreidel, "children just like you used toys like this to fool wicked old King

Antiochus." The top dances across the floor and hits Jacques's shoes. Jacques picks up the dreidel and looks at it.

"That wicked king said no children would be allowed to study Torah," says the teacher. "But do you think that stopped the children?"

"Noooo!" cries the class.

"Of course not," says the teacher. "The children studied anyway. And when the king's soldiers came near, the children pretended to be playing an innocent game of dreidel."

The teacher passes bags of peanuts. Jacques puts twenty peanuts in front of him to bet with. He also sets some in his lap to munch on while the class plays dreidel.

"A Hebrew letter is printed on each of the four sides of a dreidel," explains the teacher. "Nun, gimmel, hay, and shin. The letters stand for words meaning 'A Great Miracle Happened There,' to remind us of the miracle of the Hanukkah oil that burned for eight days."

Each child tosses one peanut into the middle of the circle. Jacques spins the top. It twirls and twirls, then falls.

"Nun!" shout his friends.

"Oh, no!" says Jacques. "Nun" means he gets nothing. He cracks a peanut shell with his teeth as the others take their turns.

On his next try, Jacques spins a gimmel. "I win!" he shouts, gathering all the peanuts from the middle. When he spins "hay," he wins half the peanuts. "Shin" means he is out of the game or has to put another peanut into the middle.

By the end of the game, Jacques has lost all twenty peanuts. He doesn't care. He will play again tonight at his cousin's house after they light the Hanukkah candles. Jacques *always* wins at his cousin's house.

Later, the rabbi comes to the classroom. "The story of Hanukkah is much like our story," he says. "Yours and mine." The rabbi's eyebrows move up and down as he talks. Jacques tries moving his.

"In the 1940s, our synagogues were seized by our enemies, the Nazis." Up and down go the rabbi's eyebrows. Up and down go Jacques's. "All our synagogues were destroyed. Unlike the Maccabees, who were able to take back their Temple, we had no buildings to return to after the war. No temple to rededicate." The rabbi raises his arms wide. "And so, we built this new synagogue."

Jacques's teacher catches him wiggling his eyebrows and stops him with a stern look. Jacques settles down and listens to the rabbi, even though he already knows the story. Every Jew in Strasbourg knows how the Nazis tried to destroy the Jews. This is why the synagogue has been built with heavy stones. This is why the massive bronze doors stand closed. As a reminder. As a precaution. As a message that this place and the spirit of the people within are stronger than the strongest enemy. As a promise that this synagogue will stand as a haven of safety and worship. Forever.

The Sixth Night: India

This has been the best Hanukkah ever! Rahmim's first twelve Hanukkahs were *nothing* compared to this. Last month he celebrated his thirteenth birthday. He became a man, a bar mitzvah, in accordance with Jewish law. This year, for the first time, Rahmim is allowed to hang a hanukkiyah on the wall next to those of his father and three brothers.

His parents have invited guests for dinner. The house fills with aunts, uncles, cousins, and friends. While the grownups visit in the house, Rahmim and the other young people play outside. It is the best season in Bombay—not hot and dry like an oven, the way it is March through June, and not hot and wet with driving monsoon rains, the way it is July through October. From November through February, the weather is perfect.

At sundown, everyone gathers inside. The living room dims in the gentle dusk. Five hanukkiyot decorate the wall. Each holds large, brightly colored glasses filled with oil. The head of the household, Rahmim's father, lights his hanukkiyah first. When all six wicks are burning, he returns the shammash to its place.

"This sixth night of Hanukkah," he says, "we celebrate the new moon, Rosh Hodesh, which begins the month of Tevet. And on this special Rosh Hodesh Tevet, I think we should also celebrate the newest man in our household. Rahmim, you may have the honor of going next."

Rahmim walks proudly to the wall and takes his time lighting his hanukkiyah. He wants this moment, when all eyes are on him, to last. When he returns the shammash to its place, his three older brothers take their turns. His sister in the United States says women there also light hanukkiyot. The idea seems strange to Rahmim. Only the men in his family have hanukkiyot. Only the men kindle the Hanukkah lights.

No one rushes on this night. On other nights, Rahmim's brothers return at all hours from school or activities. His mother and father often have to work late at the clinic. But for the eight nights of Hanukkah, everyone in the family is home by sundown. The holiday is a time for the family to be together, in their own home or in the homes of relatives or friends. No work is to be done while the Hanukkah lights burn. For two or three hours, there is nothing to do but visit.

Rahmim sits on the floor and talks to his cousins. All around them the silver and gold threads in the women's saris catch the Hanukkah lights and shimmer like raindrops. Rahmim tries to imagine how the room will look on the eighth night, when all five hanukkiyot will glow with nine lights each.

He lies back and listens to the gentle murmurs of conversations. It is good to be a man. But it is also scary. Rahmim is that much nearer the time when he will marry and leave his parents' house to start his own. His hanukkiyah will go with him, of course. And, in time, his hanukkiyah will be joined by those of his children, until they, too, leave to make their own homes. So it has been. And so it will be. Forever.

The Seventh Night: Morocco

Raquel and her mother join the other women talking and laughing on the way to the rabbi's house. Raquel looks for her friends. Are they excited, too?

All eight nights of Hanukkah are special for the women because they do no household work while the Hanukkah lights burn. Even the dinner dishes must wait two hours until the last bit of light flickers and dies. But this, the seventh night, is the most special of all.

The rabbi's wife welcomes them. Raquel and her mother settle into large pillows on the floor and wait for the rest of the women to arrive. A bronze hanukkiyah hangs on the wall above them. It is like the hanukkiyah in Raquel's home, which has been passed down for many generations. Five hands are raised in peace. Two doves fly to the shammash. Each night, oil is poured into the holders and wicks are set inside. This night's oil is almost gone, and only the tiniest dots of light still glow.

At last, everyone has arrived. It is time to begin. The women of Morocco are gifted storytellers. On this night, their stories honor the brave women who lived in the time of the Maccabees.

"And King Antiochus tried to force Hannah's seven sons to eat food forbidden by Jewish law," says Raquel's Aunt Miriam. "But Hannah and her sons refused, even to the youngest boy, barely three years old." The women around Raquel murmur and nod. "The evil king killed each son, and Hannah in her grief threw herself to her death. On this day, we honor the pain and bravery of all those who have kept the Torah in the face of danger."

Raquel is frightened by the story and squeezes her mother's hand. Another woman tells the story of Judith. "And she knew she must stop Holofernes, the evil general. For it was he who carried out the wicked laws of the king." The women hiss. "Using her rare beauty to get into his tent, Judith fed Holofernes cheese to make him thirsty. He drank much wine and, when he fell asleep, Judith killed him with his own sword and brought his head to her people."

"Ohhhh," says Raquel, making a face. Her mother smiles and gives her a gentle hug.

"When the enemy soldiers saw the bloody head of the mighty Holofernes, they ran away and left the Jews in peace."

The women clap their hands loudly for the storyteller as well as for the courage of Judith. Then it is time to gather in the kitchen, where a pot of oil heats on the stove. Twists of sweet dough are dropped into the bubbling oil and quickly puff into beignets. The hot pastries are scooped up and drained, then sprinkled with sugar. They are set out on the table next to the cheese dishes, which are served in Judith's honor. Glasses of tea are passed to wash everything down. And all the while, the women tell stories of their ancestors. Raquel smiles proudly as the name of the great matriarch Rachel is spoken.

The rabbi returns home from the synagogue where he and the men have been praying. The women prepare to go. Raquel wraps two beignets to bring to her father and takes one to eat on the way home. She and her friends run ahead of their mothers and chatter about the stories they heard. Would they have been as brave as Judith? Could they have been as strong as Hannah? Raquel is proud to be descended from such a tradition. It is wonderful that the seventh night of Hanukkah has been dedicated to women. Forever.

The Eighth Night: The Soviet Union

Anna can't sit still. All day she has waited for Grandfather to return.

"Soviet Jews are forgetting Hanukkah," he had said, wrapping his wool scarf around his neck. "Too many people have never seen it celebrated." He pulled the warm fur of his hat down over his ears. "I will ask our friends and relatives to come here for a Hanukkah party."

That had been after breakfast. Now it is nearly dark. Where can he be?

"Don't be so gloomy," says Natasha, making a funny face at her little sister. "Grandfather does not really think anyone will come to his party."

"They will come," says Anna.

"No. It will be like last year. People are either too afraid to be seen celebrating or they simply don't care about Hanukkah. You'll see."

"This year might be different," Anna says, angry that her sister does not even *hope*. But when Grandfather comes home, the look on his face tells them there will be no party.

Natasha opens the cupboard where the hanukkiyah is stored. The hanukkiyah was given to them by a London family on vacation in Moscow. An American student brought this year's candles. Sheets of Hanukkah music were a gift from a Swedish rabbi. Anna wishes the Soviet Union would allow a shop where Jews could buy such wonderful things.

Natasha takes out the hanukkiyah and sets it on the table. "Cover the window," says Mother. "There's no need for people to know our business."

Anna pulls the curtains shut so no one can look in. It's not exactly against the law to observe Hanukkah. But the government doesn't like people having religious ceremonies. It's wiser to celebrate in private. Anna opens the box of candles and takes out the last nine. She and Natasha put them into the hanukkiyah the way Grandfather taught them—from right to left, the way Hebrew is read. Candles will be lit from left to right, to honor the newest night's candle first.

There is a painting of Jerusalem on the candle box. Anna touches it slowly. Her best friend has moved to Jerusalem, and she misses her. A few times now, Anna has heard her parents talk about Israel in soft whispers. Will they, too, petition to leave the Soviet Union? Anna would like to see her friend again, but it scares her to think of leaving her home. She will save the box with the picture of Jerusalem. Only the most special things will be kept inside.

After the lighting of the candles and the blessing, Grandfather sits in his favorite chair and tells Anna and Natasha about a little girl named Anne Frank. "She, also, was not supposed to observe Hanukkah," he says. "But she did. Hiding from the Nazis in a tiny attic, making the few candles they had last all eight nights, Anne Frank and her family celebrated Hanukkah and prayed for the freedom to be Jews."

Grandfather looks tired. He closes his eyes and rubs them with his fingers. When he opens them, Anna sees the glint of tears. She rests her hand on his.

"There are Jews in other parts of the world," he says, "whose governments don't deny them the right to worship as they please. Jews who, this very night, celebrate Hanukkah right out in the open."

Anna listens and wonders at such a miracle. Imagine! To be able to light the candles of freedom without fear. Forever.

Glossary

Ark The holy cabinet in a synagogue in which the Torah scrolls are housed.

Bar mitzvah A Jewish boy who has completed his thirteenth year. Also, the ceremony recognizing the young boy's coming of age. (Girls come of age at twelve and are called bat mitzvahs.)

Bimah A raised platform, like a stage or pulpit, usually found at the front of the synagogue. The ark is on the bimah.

Bubbe, Zayde Yiddish for Grandma and Grandpa. The Yiddish language is a mixture of German, Hebrew, Aramaic, and Slavic words.

Dreidel A toy spinning top decorated with four Hebrew letters.

Hanukkiyah, hanukkiyot (pl.) A special candle holder (menorah) used only on Hanukkah. It has space for the eight lights of Hanukkah plus the shammash light.

Jerusalem The capital of the state of Israel and spiritual home of several religions.

Kislev The third month of the Jewish calendar. It corresponds to November–December. (Hanukkah begins on the twenty-fifth of Kislev.)

Menorah A candle holder. The seven-branched menorah is the emblem of the modern state of Israel.

Purim A festive holiday celebrated with costumes and noisemakers, Purim commemorates an unsuccessful plot to kill all the Jews of Persia. The story of Purim is told in the Bible, in the Book of Esther.

Rachel The wife of Jacob and one of the four matriarchs of Israel.

Rosh Hodesh Rosh Hodesh means "new moon." (A new moon begins each month in the Jewish calendar.)

Sabbath The seventh day of the week, called Shabbat in Hebrew, is set aside as a day of physical rest and spiritual joy. The Sabbath is from sundown Friday to sundown Saturday.

Shammash, shammashim (pl.) Shammash means servant. On Hanukkah, the shammash light is used to kindle all the other lights in the hanukkiyah. It is set apart in some way from the other lights.

Tevet The fourth month of the Jewish calendar. It corresponds to December–January.

Torah, scrolls The Torah contains the first five books of the Hebrew Bible. Rather than being written on separate pages, the Torah is handwritten on a long strip of animal parchment which is rolled to a new passage each week. At the end of the year, the Torah is rerolled, and the readings begin again.

Twelve tribes of Israel Ancient Israelites belonged to one of twelve tribes. Each tribe was named for a son of the patriarch Jacob, and each occupied a different territory.

Bibliography

Block, Abraham P. *The Biblical and Historical Background of Jewish Customs and Ceremonies.* New York: KTAV Publishing House, 1980.

Bridger, David, ed. *The New Jewish Encyclopedia.* New York: Behrman House, 1962.

Chiel, Kinneret. *The Complete Book of Hanukkah.* New York: Friendly House, 1959.

Drucker, Malka. *Hanukkah: Eight Nights, Eight Lights.* New York: Holiday House, 1980.

Epstein, Morris. *All About Jewish Holidays and Customs.* New York: KTAV Publishing House, 1959.

Gamoran, Mamie. *Days and Ways.* Cincinnati: UAHC, 1941.

Goldwurm, Hersh. *Chanukah, Its History, Observance, and Significance: A Presentation Based upon Talmudic and Traditional Sources.* History and Laws by Hersh Goldwurm. Ritual and Insight by Meir Zlotowitz. Overview by Nosson Scherman. Brooklyn, N.Y.: Mesorah Publications, 1969.

Goodman, Philip. *The Hanukkah Anthology.* Philadelphia: Jewish Publication Society of America, 1976.

Posner, Raphael, ed. *Junior Judaica/Encyclopaedia Judaica for Youth.* Jerusalem: Keter Publishing House, 1982.

Rockland, Mae Shafter. *The Hanukkah Book.* New York: Schocken Books, 1975.

Roth, Cecil, ed. *Encyclopaedia Judaica.* Jerusalem: Keter Publishing House, 1972.

Singer, Isadore, ed. *The Jewish Encyclopedia.* New York: Funk and Wagnalls, 1925.

Stillman, Norman A. *The Jews of Arab Lands.* Philadelphia: The Jewish Publication Society of America, 1979.

Hanukkah: Eight Lights around the World is Susan Sussman's ninth book for young people. Other books published by Albert Whitman are *Hippo Thunder; There's No Such Thing as a Chanukah Bush, Sandy Goldstein; Casey the Nomad;* and *Lies (People Believe) about Animals*. Sue lives in Evanston, Illinois, with her husband, Barry. They have three children: Rachael, Sy, and Aaron.

Judith Friedman lives in Western Springs, Illinois, with her husband, David, and their two cats, Adele and Amanda. She has been drawing and painting since the age of six, when she began art lessons in her native Paris. Judith has also illustrated *The Bad Dream, At Daddy's on Saturdays*, and *Adoption Is for Always*. When she is not drawing, she likes to refinish the antique furniture she collects and to sail on the family boat, *Beau Rêve*.